CANCER
DOESN'T
ALWAYS WIN

PRAISE FOR "CANCER DOESN'T ALWAYS WIN"

"Cancer Doesn't Always Win: A Comprehensive Guide to Beating Breast & Ovarian Cancer provides its readers with relevant, evidence-based data that enlightens and empowers the reader with the information necessary to prevent, affect, and live beyond the diagnosis."

– Dr. Terri Murdaugh-Johnson, MD, FAAP

Lead Physician,
Pediatric Associates in West Palm Beach Florida

"An informative and inspirational text that will be an invaluable resource for those diagnosed with breast and ovarian cancers. Colletta's passion and expertise in the subject matter clearly comes across."

– Dr. Aminah A. Keats, ND, FABNO

Former Director of Naturopathic Medicine
Cancer Treatment Centers of America

CANCER DOESN'T ALWAYS WIN

A Comprehensive Guide
to Beating Breast & Ovarian Cancer

COLLETTA BRABHAM-ORR, MPH

purposely
created
PUBLISHING

CANCER DOESN'T ALWAYS WIN
Copyright © 2015 Colletta Orr

Published by: Purposely Created Publishing Group™

Printed in the United States of America

ISBN (ebook) 978-1-942838-51-7
ISBN (paperback) 978-1-942838-50-0

Special discounts are available on bulk quantity purchases
by book clubs, associations and special interest groups.
For details email: sales@publishyourgift.com
or call (888) 949-6228.

For information logon to:
www.PublishYourGift.com

In Loving Memory of

My Grandmother Jannie Leigh Brabham,
and *My Great-Grandmother Katie Moss.*

These two extraordinary women are my motivation for becoming a cancer research scientist and for writing this book. My great-grandmother Katie was diagnosed with breast cancer at the age of 41 and passed away at age 42, and my grandmother Jannie was diagnosed with ovarian cancer at the age of 66 and passed away at the age of 67. Both mother and daughter were diagnosed with cancers that primarily affect women. For this reason, I decided to learn everything that I could about breast and ovarian cancers.

I wrote this book to give women a resource to reduce the risk of developing these diseases and for living a healthy life beyond cancer.

I couldn't save my grandmothers, but my hope is to save someone else's mother, grandmother, aunt, or sister.

TABLE OF CONTENTS

Dedication   vii

Author's Note   1

Introduction   7

1 Breast Cancer   9

2 Living With Cancer:
   Creating a New Normal   21

3 Breast Cancer in Men   31

4 What is Ovarian Cancer?   35

5 The Link Between Breast & Ovarian Cancer   49

6 Healthy Lifestyle & Nutrition   55

7 Additional Factors   59

8 How Can We Protect Our Daughters From
   Breast Cancer?   65

9 Ten Foods That Can Reduce The Risk of
   Breast & Ovarian Cancer   71

10 How to Get The Most of Your Doctor Visit   77

11 Living Beyond Breast or Ovarian Cancer . .   81

SURVIVOR STORIES   97

    Shetabia Morgan-Putman   99

    Dawn Smith   107

    Dewanda Mitchell   115

Conclusion   121

Resources & Support   125

References   127

About the Author   129

NOTE FROM THE AUTHOR

Breast and ovarian cancers have significantly affected my family. My maternal grandmother died from ovarian cancer, and my maternal great-grandmother died from breast cancer. They both died at relatively young ages, 67 and 42 years old, respectively.

My great-grandmother died before I was born. My grandmother and I, on the other hand, were very close. Like many grandmothers, she was the stitch that held our family together, a woman as kind and humble as one would expect a grandmother to be. I was a daily part of her life when she was first diagnosed with ovarian cancer, and yet it still happened so fast. She was diagnosed in May and died in April of the following year. She had had a complete hysterectomy in May, and her oncologist assured us that he had gotten all of the cancer.

My grandmother went through a few months of chemotherapy, and we thought all was well. However, by January her health worsened, and we couldn't understand why. She had to be hospitalized quite a bit. On one particular occasion, I spent the entire day with her at the hospital, and when her doctor came in, she was asleep. He checked his chart and took her vital signs and proceeded to walk out of her room. I followed him into the hallway to get an update on my grandmother's condition. I really couldn't understand why her health was not improving after the surgery and chemotherapy. I asked her doctor how my grandmother was doing and when could she go home. He said to me, "She is as well as can be expected." I said, "What do you mean?" He said, "Jannie didn't tell you that she has cancer all over her body?" At that moment, I went into shock. My heart broke into a million pieces. I felt totally blindsided by the news.

I was the first person in my family to hear this revelation. I then had to make a very difficult phone call to my mother. I called her and explained what the doctor had said. While I was on the phone, the doctor passed me, and I put him on the phone with my mother so he could confirm what I had told her. My grandmother had known that her condition was terminal for a few months, but she had chosen not to tell us. That day changed my life and remains a day that I will never forget.

The next day, my grandmother got another visit from the doctor, who asked her if she would like to continue the blood thinners she was using. He gave her the option, knowing that it wouldn't significantly affect the outcome of her illness. She nodded that she would like to continue. The doctor wrote down a few more notes and continued his rounds with his other patients. At that point, my grandmother knew that I was aware of her condition. She was naturally a quiet person, but now she seemed very sad and depressed. She said to me in a very low voice, "Why did all of this have to happen to me?"

My grandmother passed away two weeks later. As I relive all of these memories, my heart breaks all over again. One thing I know for sure is that when you lose a loved one, you never get over losing them; you just learn how to live without them. After my grandmother died, I sought answers. What is ovarian cancer? Where does it come from? Why hadn't I heard of this form of cancer before? When I was in college, I majored in biology, not only because I had always had a strong interest in the sciences, but also because I wanted to understand the vicious ovarian cancer that stole my best friend. After my undergraduate studies, I got a position at Georgetown University Lombardi Cancer Center in Washington, DC. There, I had my first experience with breast and ovarian cancer research. During that time, I wanted to learn as much as I could about ovarian cancer, and as I got into my research, I discovered that breast and ovarian cancers were genetically linked. That was an "aha" moment for me. It was all coming together. My great-grandmother had breast cancer, and her daughter (my grandmother) had ovarian cancer. There was the genetic link. I wanted to learn and understand more.

After Georgetown, I secured a position at The National Cancer Institute, where I continued my research. I went on to present my work at national conferences throughout the United States. This is where my passion for breast and ovarian cancers awareness originated. Since then, I have become a huge advocate for breast and ovarian cancers awareness. I make sure that my mother gets the necessary check-ups and screenings since her maternal genes make her high-risk. I feel that if all women have the information they need, they can make informed decisions about their health and live longer lives. Hopefully, they won't overlook the small things that are possible symptoms of something much more significant. My research has changed my life positively in so many ways, and I hope that it will do the same for others. KNOW YOUR FAMILY'S HISTORY!

In 1995, President Barack Obama lost his mother to ovarian cancer. She she was 52 years old. Here's what he told Prevention magazine in an exclusive statement:

"Experiences like my mother's are far too common. Ovarian cancer still claims more lives than any other reproductive cancer. That's why my administration is committed to developing effective screening, improving treatments, and defeating this disease.

While we continue to promote awareness of ovarian cancer and advance its diagnosis and treatment, it falls to all of us to look out for the women we love. I encourage all women, especially those over age fifty-five or with a family history, to protect your health by understanding risk factors and discussing possible symptoms with your health care provider. And talk to your loved ones: Encourage them to gather the facts and protect their health."

INTRODUCTION

Cancer affects each population in different ways. Unfortunately, this means that minority groups in the United States continue to bear a greater cancer burden than whites. Much of this difference is because of poverty and a lack of access to prevention or detection services and quality treatment. For instance, African Americans and Hispanics in the United States have higher poverty rates than whites and are less likely to have health insurance, making it harder for them to get the care they need.

The truth is that breast cancer is a leading cancer diagnosis in women, and ovarian cancer is the deadliest cancer in women. Additionally, these cancers often run in families. Thus, your family history can help determine how high your risk is for breast and ovarian cancers.

One in eight women (12 percent) will develop breast cancer. The lifetime risk for women who have a family history of breast cancer but no known genetic mutation is approximately 20–30 percent. The risk for women with a genetic mutation inherited from either parent is even higher at approximately 60-87 percent.

One in 67 women (1–2 percent) will develop ovarian cancer. The lifetime risk for women who have a family history of ovarian cancer but no known genetic mutation is approximately 4–7 percent, and the risk for women with a genetic mutation passed down from either parent is approximately 20–54 percent.

For some, these cancers seem to run in the family. Sometimes it's because of mutated genes (the BRCA1 or BRCA2 genes) that dramatically increase the risk of developing cancer. These genes are passed down from one's mother or father. Women who carry these genes can have up to an 87 percent lifetime risk of developing breast cancer and up to a 54 percent lifetime risk of developing ovarian cancer.

CHAPTER 1

∿∿∿∿∿∿∿∿∿∿∿∿∿∿∿∿∿∿∿∿∿∿∿∿∿∿∿∿∿∿

BREAST CANCER

Breast cancer occurs when normal breast cells grow and reproduce out of control, turning into cancerous (malignant) cells. These abnormal cells grow so much that they fill the ducts (ductal cancer) or the lobules (lobular cancer) of the breast. The lobules are glands that produce breast milk, and the ducts are the passageways that carry the milk from the lobules to the nipple.

Female breast cancer is the most commonly diagnosed cancer among all races, yet mortality rates differ by race and ethnicity, and early detection numbers falter among minorities. Breast cancer is the second-most common cause of cancer death for all women, with the exception of Hispanics, for whom it is the number one cause of death.

The American Cancer Society's estimates for breast cancer in the United States for 2014 are:

- About 232,670 new cases of invasive breast cancer will be diagnosed in women.

- About 62,570 new cases of carcinoma *in situ* (CIS) will be diagnosed. (CIS is non-invasive and is the earliest form of breast cancer.)

- About 40,000 women will die from breast cancer.

Death rates from breast cancer have been declining since 1989, with larger decreases in women younger than 50. These decreases are believed to be the result of earlier detection through screening and increased awareness, as well as from better treatment.

At this time, there are more than 2.8 million breast cancer survivors in the United States. (This includes women still being treated and those who have completed treatment.)

What are the Causes of Breast Cancer?

Experts are not certain what causes breast cancer. It is hard to say why one person develops the disease while another does not. We know that some risk factors can affect a woman's likelihood of developing breast cancer. These risk factors are as follows:

- Getting older – The older a woman gets, the higher her risk of developing breast cancer. Age, too, is a risk factor. Over 80 percent of all female breast cancers occur among women who are over 50 years old (after menopause).

- Genetics – Women with a close relative who has or has had breast or ovarian cancer are more likely to develop breast cancer. However, if two close family members develop the disease, it does not necessarily mean they shared the genes that make them more vulnerable because breast cancer is a relatively common cancer.

The majority of breast cancers are not hereditary.

- Women who carry the BRCA1 and BRCA2 genes have a considerably higher risk of developing breast and/or ovarian cancer. These genes can

11

be inherited. TP53, another gene, is also linked to greater breast cancer risk.

- A history of breast cancer – Women who have had breast cancer, even non-invasive cancer, are more likely to develop the disease again compared to women with no history of the disease.

- Dense breast tissue – Women with more dense breast tissue have a greater chance of developing breast cancer.

- Estrogen exposure – Women who started menstruating earlier or who entered menopause later than usual have a higher risk of developing breast cancer. This is because their bodies have been exposed to estrogen for longer, starting when their periods began and dropping dramatically during menopause.

- Obesity – Post-menopausal obese and overweight women may have a higher risk of developing breast cancer. Experts say that there are higher levels of estrogen in obese menopausal women, which may be the cause of the higher risk.

- Height – Taller-than-average women have a slightly greater likelihood of developing breast cancer than shorter-than-average women. Experts are not sure why.

- Alcohol consumption – The more alcohol a woman drinks, the higher her risk of developing breast cancer. The Mayo Clinic says that if a woman wants to drink, she should not exceed one alcoholic beverage per day.

- Radiation exposure – Undergoing X-rays and CT scans may slightly raise a woman's risk of developing breast cancer.

Diagnosing Breast Cancer

Women are usually diagnosed with breast cancer after a routine breast cancer screening, or after detecting certain signs and symptoms and consulting their doctors.

If a woman detects any breast cancer signs and symptoms, she should speak to her doctor immediately. Often, a primary care physician will carry out a physical exam and then refer the patient to a specialist if he or she thinks further assessment is needed.

Below are examples of diagnostic tests and procedures for breast cancer:

Breast exam – The physician will check both of the patient's breasts, looking for lumps and other possible abnormalities, such as inverted nipples, nipple discharge, or changes in breast shape. The patient will be asked to sit or stand with her arms in different positions, such as above her head and by her sides.

X-ray (mammogram) – This is commonly used for breast cancer screening. If the doctor finds anything unusual, he or she may order a diagnostic mammogram.

Many controversies regarding breast cancer screening have developed over the last few years. Experts, professional bodies, and patient groups cannot agree on when mammography screening should start and how often it should occur. Some say routine screening should start when the woman is 40 years old, others insist that 50 is the best age, and a few believe that only high-risk groups should have routine screenings.

Overcoming the Fear of Breast Cancer

If you're scared that one day you will hear someone tell you you have breast cancer, you've got plenty of company. Breast cancer is the most feared cancer among women. Sometimes, the root of the fear isn't the word "cancer"; for many women, the fear is of treating cancer, such as surgical complications and medication side effects. Perhaps you've been through a breast cancer diagnosis with someone close to you and know how difficult it can be.

While these fears are understandable, the danger is that some women are so overwhelmed with anxiety that they postpone screenings like breast exams and mammograms, or even skip them altogether, for fear of bad news. Yet these are the very examinations that can help save lives by finding cancer early when it's most treatable.

Women who are newly diagnosed with breast cancer face a different set of fears as they go through various stages of anxiety and acceptance. Many are in denial at first, which can quickly turn into anger or a feeling like the world has been turned upside down. Some women wonder what they have done to deserve the diagnosis and are unsure about recovery. Eventually, reality sets in

15

and treatment begins, which is when many women feel better and more in control of their disease, because they are actively fighting it.

Those who survive breast cancer struggle with the fear that their cancer might return. Every post-treatment checkup, mammogram, and blood test is full of anxiety, as is waiting for the results.

You can't let breast cancer blindside you!

Advances in methods of detection and treatments have transformed breast cancer from what had been considered a dreaded disease—what some perceived as a death sentence—to one that most women can and do beat. In fact, when breast cancer is found at its earliest, most treatable stage, a majority of women (98 percent) will go on to live full, healthy lives after treatment. This is why it's important to keep up with recommended screenings and exams.

If you're 40 years or older, you should get a routine mammogram. In addition to the fear of getting a suspicious mammogram result, you may also be embarrassed to bare your breasts, or perhaps you'd rather avoid the discomfort that comes with positioning and squeezing the breasts to take the image. But temporary uneasiness and minor discomfort are small prices to pay for early detection.

If you're new to the task, ask the technician to explain what to expect. Be sure to find out when you can expect the results, so you aren't consumed with worry if you don't hear right away. If you are asked to come back and repeat the test, don't be alarmed. The film may have been difficult to read. If your doctor does notice something suspicious on your mammogram, he or she may order a biopsy to remove a sample of breast tissue and examine it for cancer. To put your mind at ease, consider that four out of five biopsies will not be cancer. Doctors are merely erring on the side of caution.

It is also important to talk with your health care provider to learn about your personal risk of developing breast cancer so you can decide how to stay on top of your breast health. While you're at it, ask about lung cancer and heart disease, too—these are the leading causes of death among women. Don't forget periodic breast self-exams, either. Many women neglect doing these for fear of ending up in the doctor's office every month with a new lump and bump, but it's important that you get to know your breasts over time so you notice any changes. Attitude and support ease anxiety.

Having breast cancer is a difficult experience. You are probably worried about the road ahead, the ways your diagnosis will affect the important relationships in your life, and your body image, not to mention your family and work obligations. Seeking emotional support and maintaining a positive attitude (as best you can) will help ease your anxieties.

☑ Here are some tips:

- Practice the art of happiness. It may be easier said than done, but try not to get weighed down with grief and worry. Boost your spirits whenever you can by meeting a friend for lunch, writing (and referring to) inspirational messages in a journal, or going for a walk in a park.

- Join a breast cancer support group where you can share your anxieties with other women going through the same challenge who have similar concerns. If you feel more comfortable chatting with others from the comfort of your home, there are safe message boards at sites like Breastcancer.org.

- Don't be afraid to express your fears to your loved ones. You're not Superwoman, and it's

18

perfectly acceptable to share the burden with others. For many women, the old adage "what doesn't kill you makes you stronger" applies.

- Take a deep breath. If you notice that your mind is swirling with worry, try meditation or deep-breathing exercises.

- Ask questions. Your mind may get ahead of you at times, so ask questions to make sure you aren't worrying unnecessarily.

- Don't let cancer define you. You had a life before cancer, and there is life after, so don't lose sight of who you are. Stay connected to the people and activities that are important to you.

CHAPTER 2

LIVING WITH CANCER: CREATING A NEW NORMAL

How many times, as a cancer survivor, have you thought it would be nice to get back to your normal life?

Many breast cancer survivors have said that living with a cancer diagnosis is like riding a rollercoaster. Each day brings new feelings, worries, and emotions, both positive and negative. Instead of constantly thinking about what life was like before your diagnosis, focus your energy on the present day.

If negative thoughts start creeping in, recognize them and then tuck them away; don't dwell on them for long. When you have a good day, be aware of what was good about it. Think about what makes you happy and brings you joy.

Create a new normal by living one day at a time.

- Be open to your emotions – Don't be afraid to feel both negative and positive emotions.

- Realize that some things are out of your control – Focus on the things you can control, and act on those instead.

- Take action to reduce stressors – Chronic stress will not help your situation. Explore relaxation and stress relief strategies such as exercise, Tai Chi, yoga, meditation, or expressive writing and art.

- Set aside 30 minutes every day for yourself – Discover new ways to bring happiness and contentment to your life.

- Try something new – Now is a great time to start an herb garden, grow orchids, take a cooking glass, or learn to dance.

The idea is to find a new normal and embrace it. Don't look back, but remember what makes you happy and recognize any new limitations. I'd love to hear your thoughts on how you create a new normal every day.

You can contact me through my website: www.collettaorr.com.

Sex After Breast Surgery

If you've just learned that you have breast cancer, your sex life may be the last thing on your mind. But as you move through surgery and treatment, it is definitely worth thinking about how you can maintain and preserve your sexuality. That's because sex is so closely tied to intimacy. Having cancer can be lonely enough; you need the touching and loving that comes from intimacy now more than ever. Plus, sexuality helps you maintain a sense of normalcy, health, and vitality, all of which are so important when dealing with a serious illness.

There's no denying that cancer, regardless of the type, can have a huge impact on your sex life. The worry and fear alone may make you less interested in sex, not to mention the side effects from treatments and the healing process after surgery.

But breast cancer brings special challenges. To many women, the breasts are an important part of their sexual identity. Even if your breast cancer was discovered early and removed with breast-conserving surgery rather than a mastectomy, studies find little difference in the cancer's effect on your sex life. The good news, however, is that women undergoing lumpectomy report fewer body image problems and greater feelings of sexual attractiveness. Unfortunately, that doesn't translate into more sex. Even women who had breast reconstruction after their mastectomies did not report an increased interest in sex.

Breast surgery, of course, is just one component of treatment. Medications designed to reduce or stop the production of estrogen in premenopausal women, such as tamoxifen or toremifene (Fareston), can cause vaginal changes, such as drier, thinner tissue that is more likely to tear and cause painful intercourse. Aromatase inhibitors, which are increasingly used in treating early breast cancer in postmenopausal women, also worsen vaginal dryness and contribute to sexual problems. Chemotherapy drugs can lead to weight gain, hair loss, and skin changes that may affect your self-esteem and reduce your libido. Plus, the intense fatigue that often comes with cancer treatment can make sex the last thing on your list.

Recognize that recovering from cancer physically, emotionally, and sexually takes time. In one survey of 50 women, a year after breast surgery, 80 percent said they either had no sexual desire or reduced sexual desire. The women found that their illness affected their relationships, with one-third saying the main cause, a lack of desire, was related to feelings of physical inadequacy.

I urge you to talk with your partner about these changes in your body and the ways they make you feel. If you don't feel like having intercourse, communicate that clearly, but let your partner know that you still love and value him or her and that you still want and need to be touched and cuddled during this phase.

One study found that women with breast cancer felt more comfortable talking about sexual problems with their partner than with a therapist. However, if you want to talk with a therapist, ask your doctor or oncology nurse for a referral to one who specializes in working with cancer patients.

You deserve a healthy sexual life as much as you deserve to be healthy.

Spouses of Breast Cancer

The physical and emotional concern for spouses of breast cancer survivors can be overwhelming. It is important for spouses of breast cancer survivors to address these needs in order to promote physical and mental health. Many of the resources listed below can help spouses who are faced with physical and emotional challenges.

☑ Tips for spouses of breast cancer survivors:

- Listen to her. Your spouse really needs someone to be there for her, and it is important that you listen and make sure she knows that you support her.

- Tell her she is beautiful. Your spouse's body has gone through many changes from breast cancer treatments. These changes can make your spouse feel unattractive, so it is important that you remind her that she is still beautiful.

- Communicate openly. It is always best to talk things over with each other rather than keep it inside. If you have something on your mind, don't be afraid to communicate your feelings with your spouse. It will make the relationship stronger.

- Schedule time for just the two of you. It may seem hard to find alone time with the constant demands of everyday life, but it is very important that you schedule time for you and your spouse. You can do anything from watching a movie to going out to eat at your favorite restaurant. Remember to schedule the activity based on your spouse's energy level and physical ability.

- Understand that there will be changes in your sexual relationship. Know that your spouse's breasts may or may not be used for sexual stimulation, and that other methods of stimulation may be necessary. Always make sure that your partner is healthy enough for sexual activity. It may benefit you to take a class that explains how the body will change sexually after breast cancer treatments.

- Let go of the need to control everything. It is important to know that you can't control every situation. One thing you can do is to try and stay positive, which may make you cope better.

- Understand that each person copes differently. Don't be upset or angry if your spouse reacts differently than you think she should to the diagnosis, treatment, and post-treatment. Not every person reacts the same way, and everyone handles things differently.

- Take care of household chores. Your spouse may not have the energy to do some of the household chores that she used to do. She would greatly appreciate the help, and it shows that you are supporting her while she is unable to do what she used to.

- Accept help when you need it. Having to handle many things at one time is hard. You may find it useful to accept help from friends or family members. Do not feel guilty about asking or accepting help, because you will need a break.

When Do You Need to Seek Help?

Right now! If you are having issues and feel like you cannot handle the stress, seek help immediately. You may feel overwhelmed, but this is perfectly normal. You should seek help whenever you need it.

We Are in This Together!

- Seek help together. Looking for help as a couple will give you a chance to hear your spouse's concerns, which will give your spouse a chance to hear yours as well. This is also a chance to strengthen your relationship.

- It's okay to cry together. You and your spouse may feel different things. Some days may be harder than others. Remember that it is perfectly fine to cry if you feel you should. Do not hide your feelings.

- Laugh together. Just laugh. Even about the little things. Laughing is a wonderful way to pass time. It is also a great way to stop thinking about cancer, even if it is only for a moment!

- Say I love you! It is important to remind your spouse that she is loved. Taking a moment to tell your spouse that she is loved can comfort her through such a difficult time. It can also help you to hear "I love you too."

CHAPTER 3

〰〰〰〰〰〰〰〰〰〰〰〰〰〰〰〰〰

BREAST CANCER IN MEN

Even though men do not have breasts like women, they do have a small amount of breast tissue. In fact, the "breasts" of an adult man are similar to the breasts of a girl before puberty, which consist of a few ducts surrounded by fat and other tissue. In girls, this tissue grows and develops in response to female hormones, but in men, who do not secrete the same amounts of these hormones, this tissue does not develop.

However, because men still have breast tissue, they can develop breast cancer. In fact, men get the same types of breast cancers that women do, although cancers involving the milk-producing and milk-storing regions of the breast are very rare.

Breast cancer in men is a very rare disease. This is possibly due to their smaller amount of breast tissue and the fact that men produce fewer hormones like estrogen, which are known to cause breast cancers in women.

There are 1,400 cases of male breast cancer per year. In fact, only about 1 percent of all breast cancers affect men.

It is very rare for a man under age 35 to get breast cancer, but the likelihood of him developing the disease increases with age. Breast cancer is most commonly diagnosed in men between the ages of 50 and 70. Beyond that, African American men appear to be at greater risk than Caucasian men. In some places in Africa, breast cancer in men is much more common. Also, college-educated professionals appear to have a higher risk than the general male population.

Men with abnormal enlargement of the breasts (called gynecomastia) in response to drug or hormone treatments, obesity, or some infections and poisons have the greatest risk for developing breast cancer. Individuals with a rare genetic disease called Klinefelter's syndrome, who often have gynecomastia as part of it, are especially prone to breast cancer.

Doctors used to think that breast cancer in men was a more severe disease than it was in women, but it now seems that for comparably advanced breast cancers, men and women have similar outcomes.

The major problem is that breast cancer is often diagnosed later in men compared to women, which may be because men are less likely to be suspicious of an abnormality in that area.

For men, symptoms are very similar to those in women. Most male breast cancers are diagnosed when a man discovers a lump on his chest. However, unlike women, men tend to go to the doctor with more severe symptoms that often include bleeding from the nipple and abnormalities in the skin above the cancer. For a large number of men, the cancer has already spread to the lymph nodes.

The same techniques, physical exams, mammograms, and biopsies (examining small samples of the tissue under a microscope) used to diagnose breast cancer in women are also used for men.

The same four treatments used to treat breast cancer in women, including surgery, radiation, chemotherapy, and hormones, are also used to treat the disease in men. As is the case with women, mastectomy is the recommended surgery for men.

Many breast cancers in men have hormone receptors, meaning they have specific sites on the cancer cells where specific hormones like estrogen can act. Therefore, hormonal treatment in men is likely to be effective.

CHAPTER 4

〰〰〰〰〰〰〰〰〰〰〰〰〰〰〰〰〰〰〰〰

WHAT IS OVARIAN CANCER?

Ovarian cancer is cancer that forms in tissues of the ovary (a pair of female reproductive glands in which the ova, or eggs, are formed). Most ovarian cancers are either ovarian epithelial carcinomas (cancer that begins in the cells on the surface of the ovary) or malignant germ cell tumors (cancer that begins in egg cells). Ovarian cancer typically progresses with no recognizable symptoms, and as a result is often diagnosed in advanced stages when it is harder to treat. About 43 percent of patients survive at least five years.

Estimated new cases and deaths from ovarian cancer in the United States in 2014 are:

New cases: 21,980   Deaths: 14,270

Every 35 minutes, a woman loses her life to ovarian cancer, making it the deadliest of all gynecologic cancers. In fact, ovarian cancer kills more women than all gynecologic cancers combined. What's most upsetting is that ovarian cancer has about a 90 percent cure rate when it is detected early! Yet less than 15 percent of women know the symptoms, and over 80 percent have never had a conversation with their doctors about this disease. Over 75 percent of women diagnosed with ovarian cancer are in the late stages of the disease, and survival rates are too depressing to even discuss.

Risk Factors

While most women with ovarian cancer do not have any known risk factors, some do exist. If a woman has one or more risk factors, she will not necessarily develop ovarian cancer; however, her risk may be higher than the average woman's.

Genetics

About 10 to 15 percent of women diagnosed with ovarian cancer have a hereditary tendency to develop the disease. The most significant risk factor for ovarian cancer is an inherited genetic mutation in one of two genes: breast cancer gene 1 (BRCA1) or breast cancer gene 2 (BRCA2). These genes are responsible for about 5 to 10 percent of all ovarian cancers. Around 20 percent of the female population carries a gene that can predispose them to ovarian cancer, and half do not have any family history of the disease. Over 80 percent of women diagnosed with ovarian cancer are over 50, although it can occur in younger women. The risk of cancer is increased for some women with a strong family history. If two or more first-degree 'blood relatives' (i.e. mother, sister, daughter) have been diagnosed with ovarian or breast cancer, particularly before the age of 50, then the risk is significantly increased.

Age

The majority of ovarian cancers occur in women over 65 years of age. A higher percentage of post-menopausal women develop ovarian cancer compared to pre-menopausal women.

High Number of Total Lifetime Ovulations

There is a link between the total number of ovulations during a woman's life and the risk of ovarian cancer.

Four principal factors influence the total:

- Never having been pregnant – Women who have never been pregnant have a higher risk of developing ovarian cancer compared to women who have been pregnant. The more times a woman is pregnant, the lower her risk.

- Never having taken the contraceptive pill – Women who have never been on the contraceptive pill have a higher risk of developing ovarian cancer compared to women who have.

- Early start of menstruation – Women who started their periods at an early age have a higher risk of developing ovarian cancer.

- Late start of menopause – Women whose menopause started later than average have a higher risk of developing ovarian cancer.

Infertility, regardless of whether a woman uses fertility drugs, also increases the risk of ovarian cancer.

Obesity

Various studies have found a link between obesity and ovarian cancer. A 2009 study found that obesity was associated with an almost 80 percent higher risk of ovarian cancer in women ages 50 to 71 who had not taken hormones after menopause.

Diabetes

Meta-analyses have shown that diabetics have a 20-55 percent increased risk of ovarian cancer compared to non-diabetics. The type of treatment that diabetics use may also affect their risk. Although the use of metformin or pioglitazone is not associated with ovarian cancer risk, insulin-users may have a slightly increased risk compared to non-users.

Reducing Risk

Women can reduce their risk of developing ovarian cancer in many ways; however, there is no absolute way to prevent the disease. This means that all women are at risk, because ovarian cancer does not strike only one ethnic or age group. A health care professional can help a woman identify ways to reduce her risk and help her decide if consultation with a genetic counselor is appropriate.

Oral Contraceptives (Birth-Control Pills)

The use of oral contraceptives decreases the risk of developing ovarian cancer, especially when used for several years. Women who use oral contraceptives for five or more years have about a 50 percent lower risk of developing ovarian cancer than women who have never used oral contraceptives.

How is ovarian cancer diagnosed?

- A vaginal-rectal pelvic examination (also called a bimanual exam) – This exam allows the ovaries to be examined from many sides. Every woman should undergo a rectal and vaginal pelvic examination at her gynecological check-up.

- Transvaginal ultrasound - This test uses sound waves to create a picture of the ovaries and can often reveal if there are masses or irregularities on the surface of the ovaries. It cannot determine if you have cancer, but it can show characteristics that give different levels of suspicion.

- CA125 blood test - This test measures the level of a certain type of protein in the blood that may increase when a cancerous tumor is present. Ovarian cancer cells produce this protein, which is elevated in more than 80 percent of women with advanced ovarian cancers and 50 percent of those with early-stage cancers. In fact, CA125 is present in half of early cancers. However, it can be elevated in benign conditions. The National Cancer Institute (NCI) does not endorse using it to screen women with ordinary risk or in the general population.

- It is very important to note that none of these tests are definitive when used in isolation. They are most effective when used in conjunction with other tests. The fact remains: the only way to confirm the presence of ovarian cancer suspected by the above tests is through a surgical biopsy of the tumor tissue.

- The Pap test is used to detect cervical cancer, NOT ovarian cancer.

If tests suggest the possibility of ovarian cancer, seek a referral to a gynecologic oncologist:

- A gynecologic oncologist is a physician who specializes in treating women with cancers of the reproductive tract.

- Gynecologic oncologists are initially trained as obstetrician/gynecologists and then undergo three to four years of specialized education in all of the effective forms of treatment for gynecologic cancers (surgery, radiation, chemotherapy, and experimental treatments) as well as the biology and pathology of gynecologic cancers.

○ ○ ○

I cannot stress enough the importance of being treated by a gynecologic oncologist. According to numerous medical studies, there are significant survival advantages for women who are treated, managed, and operated on by a gynecologic oncologist.

- Gynecologic oncologists are five times more likely to completely remove ovarian tumors during surgery.

- 80 percent of ovarian cancer patients receive inadequate surgical debulking and staging from non-gynecologic oncology surgeons.

- Survival rates and outcomes vastly improve with gynecologic oncologists.

You can find a gynecologic oncologist in your area by calling The Gynecologic Cancer Foundation toll-free hotline at 1-800-444-4441, or by visiting them online at www.wcn.org.

Living with Ovarian Cancer

Women living with ovarian cancer may undergo a unique journey through treatment and survivorship.

Recurrence is common with ovarian cancer, which means that close follow-up evaluations and monitoring are important. This may include a pelvic exam, X-rays, CT or MRI scans, and blood tests to monitor the tumor marker CA-125. Recurrence may also mean undergoing treatment with chemotherapy each time a recurrence is detected. Additionally, a clinical trial can be an option for treatment. It's also not uncommon to ask for a second opinion regarding treatment recommendations.

If you are a woman living with recurrent ovarian cancer, you have unique needs. Living with uncertainty may be the most difficult aspect of survivorship.

☑ You may find support by trying these strategies:

- Talk with other ovarian cancer survivors.

- Explore mind-body techniques to deal with stress and anxiety, including meditation, yoga, and exercise.

- Learn the physical signs of recurrence, including pelvic pain, bloating, changes in bowel or bladder function, lack of energy, and back pain. Keep a journal of your symptoms to track any changes.

- Take time for yourself – focus on healthy choices in the areas of your life you can control.

Take Our Quiz!

Ovarian cancer is the leading cause of death from gynecologic cancers in the United States, and the fifth leading cause of cancer death among American women. There is no better time than now to learn as much as you can about ovarian cancer symptoms and prevention. Take our quiz, test your knowledge, and be sure to share it with a friend!

1. Ovarian cancer symptoms include:

  (a) Pelvic and/or abdominal pain, bloating, or a feeling of fullness

  (b) Severe headaches

  (c) Shooting pains in the arms and legs

  (d) Extreme sweating

2. Risk factors for ovarian cancer include:

  (a) Inherited gene mutations

  (b) Being under the age of 40 with a personal or family history of breast cancer

  (c) All of the above

3. Both breast and ovarian cancers can be caused by gene mutations.

(a) True

(b) False

4. A prophylactic oophorectomy is:

(a) The surgical removal of the cervix

(b) The removal of both ovaries and tubes for prevention of ovarian/tubal cancer in extremely high-risk patients

(c) A diagnostic and therapeutic procedure where a small amount of radiation is directed at the cancerous tissue

(d) An instrument used to view the ovaries

5. How is ovarian cancer usually treated?

(a) Cytoreductive surgery and surgical staging (removal of ovarian tumors)

(b) Chemotherapy

(c) Radiation therapy when appropriate

(d) All of the above

Answers

1. (A)

Abdominal bloating, pelvic and/or abdominal pain, and/or a feeling of fullness are all symptoms of ovarian cancer, in addition to vague but persistent and unexplained gastrointestinal complaints, such as gas, nausea, and indigestion; unexplained change in bowel habits (constipation or diarrhea); unexplained weight gain or loss; frequency and/or urgency of urination; unusual fatigue; shortness of breath; and new and unexplained abnormal postmenopausal vaginal bleeding.

2. (C)

All of these factors make you at higher risk than the average woman. Several factors may increase your risk of ovarian cancer. Having one or more of these risk factors doesn't mean that you're sure to develop ovarian cancer, but your risk may be higher than the average woman's.

3. (A)

Both breast and ovarian cancers can be caused by mutations in the BRCA1 and BRCA2 genes. Women with a family history of breast and ovarian cancers, or a personal history for either, particularly if diagnosed before age 50, should be aware of an increased risk for the other.

4. (B)

Prophylactic oophorectomy, or risk-reducing salpingo-oophorectomy, is the removal of both ovaries and tubes for prevention of ovarian/tubal cancer in extremely high-risk patients.

5. (D)

All of the listed options are used to treat ovarian cancer. A gynecologic oncologist must determine treatment for recurrent ovarian cancer.

CHAPTER 5

THE LINK BETWEEN BREAST & OVARIAN CANCER

Cancer is common. Almost everybody has at least one relative with the disease. Most cancers happen by chance or due to environmental exposures. However, some people have an increased chance of developing certain types of cancer, such as breast or ovarian cancer, because of a genetic mutation. About 5-10 percent of all breast cancer cases and 10 percent of ovarian cancer cases are due to a BRCA mutation.

Gene mutation means one has a higher cancer risk. Some people are not born with normal BRCA genes—they inherit a mutation (an abnormal genetic change) in one of their BRCA1 or BRCA2 genes. Since they lack backup protection, any damage to the remaining normal BRCA gene in either set will lead to cancer.

People born with a BRCA gene mutation carry a much higher risk of developing breast and ovarian cancer than those born with two normal sets of genes.

The likelihood that breast and ovarian cancers are associated with BRCA1 or BRCA2 is highest in families with a history of multiple cases of breast cancer, cases of both breast and ovarian cancer, cancer at early ages, families in which one or more family members has two primary cancers (original tumors at different sites), or people of an Ashkenazi (Eastern European) Jewish background. However, not every woman in such families has a mutation in BRCA1 or BRCA2, and not every cancer in such families is linked to mutations in these genes.

The link between breast cancer and ovarian cancer has to do with the parallel risks of developing either cancer. Researchers have discovered that women who develop breast cancer have an increased risk of developing ovarian cancer later in life. Similarly, women who develop ovarian cancer have an increased risk of developing breast cancer later in life.

The relationship between these increased risks is based on hereditary factors. Women with a family history of breast cancer or ovarian cancer have an increased risk of developing either cancer. These risks increase to varying degrees depending on which cancer the family has a history of, the particulars of the family history, the time period in which the woman develops the cancer, and the type of cancer the woman develops. For example, women who develop breast cancer before age 40 are three times more likely to develop ovarian cancer later in life than women who do not develop breast cancer. However, women who develop breast cancer before age 40 and have a family history of ovarian cancer are 17 times more likely to develop ovarian cancer later in life.

These increased risks of developing breast cancer and ovarian cancer are partly explained by the inherited mutations of two particular genes: BRCA1 and BRCA2. Both of these genes belong to a larger class of genes known as tumor suppressors and are essential for repairing damaged DNA. Researchers have discovered that these genes mutate in some women, which substantially increases the risk of developing breast and ovarian cancers. Women with normal functioning BRCA1 and BRCA2 genes have about a 12 percent risk of developing breast cancer and about a two percent risk of developing ovarian cancer by age 70. In contrast, women with a mutated BRCA1 or BRCA2 gene have up to an 85 percent risk of developing breast cancer and up to a 50 percent risk of developing ovarian cancer by age 70.

A BRCA mutation can be passed down from one's mother or father. BRCA mutations are inherited in a dominant fashion, which means one copy of an altered BRCA1 or BRCA2 gene in each cell is sufficient to increase the chance of developing certain cancers. It is important to remember that not everyone who inherits mutations in these genes will develop cancer.

When a person with a BRCA mutation has children, each child has a 50 percent chance (1 in 2) of inheriting the BRCA mutation and a 50 percent chance of inheriting the working BRCA gene copy. The children who do inherit the BRCA mutation have an increased chance of developing cancer and can also pass the gene on to their children. Those who inherit their parents' working BRCA gene copy cannot pass the mutation on to their children. In cases where a BRCA mutation is *not* passed onto a child, family history of cancer is still prevalent. It is important to note that they are still at risk of developing cancer, just not due to a BRCA mutation. Experts believe that research will uncover more gene mutations in the future, but the link between breast and ovarian cancers and heredity is already established.

Signs that there may be a BRCA mutation in you or your family include:

- You or a family member has been diagnosed with breast cancer at an earlier age than usual (before age 50).

- You or a family member has developed two or more separate cancers (for example, a woman who develops breast cancer and later, ovarian cancer).

- Two or more of your relatives in the same bloodline have been diagnosed with breast or ovarian cancer.

- There is a known BRCA mutation in your family. (Thus, there *is* a BRCA mutation in your family, which means you *may* have a BRCA mutation.)
- There is a family history of breast or ovarian cancer and your family is of Ashkenazi Jewish descent.

To determine whether genetic testing for the presence of a BRCA mutation is right for you, make an appointment to speak with a genetic counselor and discuss your family health history.

It is important to remember that many women without a family history develop breast cancer each year. Women should not feel falsely reassured by a negative family history.

CHAPTER 6

HEALTHY LIFESTYLE & NUTRITION

Keep your body on track by committing to these healthy habits:

- Limit your fat intake. Research shows a modest decrease in invasive breast cancer in women who eat a low-fat diet. Fill up on cancer-fighting foods like fruits and vegetables, and eat red meat sparingly.

- Maintain a healthy body weight. There's a clear link between obesity and breast cancer because fatty tissue produces excess estrogen. Maintaining a healthy weight is one of the most important actions you can take to reduce your risk.

- Make exercise a part of your daily life. Regular exercise for 30 minutes or more on most days can reduce your risk of developing breast cancer. Plus, it has many other benefits like lowering your risk for heart disease and reducing stress.

- Cut back on cocktails. There appears to be a link between alcohol and breast cancer, although scientists don't really know how strong. Stay on the safe side and limit your alcohol consumption (that includes beer, wine, and liquor) to one drink per day, or eliminate it completely.

- Don't smoke. While there is limited research suggesting a link between cigarettes and breast and ovarian cancers, there is a direct link between tobacco use and many other cancers, and not just lung or oral cancers.

Nutrition

Research has shown that certain foods can actually decrease your risk of developing cancer. These cancer-fighting foods are not only nutritious, they are inexpensive, too, and provide a natural way to take action and manage health.

☑ Here's what to look for when you head to the grocery store:

- **Vitamin D:** Vitamin D is known to reduce the incidence of breast and ovarian cancers by slowing the growth of cancer cells. Our sun is the primary source of vitamin D, but we also know that sun exposure can be dangerous. So the best way to get more vitamin D in your diet is by eating fatty fish (such as salmon). Vitamin D can also be found in milk, fortified cereal, orange juice, and eggs. Have your levels checked at your primary care physician's office, and if you are low, you should consider taking supplements.

- **Vitamin A:** Researchers have found that this powerful vitamin can actually reduce the risk of developing breast cancer in those with a family history of the disease. Carrots, sweet potatoes, dried herbs, and leafy greens are all rich in vitamin A.

- **Vitamin E:** This vitamin has been clinically proven to slow the growth of cancer cells in the ovaries by reducing the production of telomerase, a ribonucleoprotein that can increase the risk of developing ovarian cancer. Foods rich in vitamin E include leafy greens such as Swiss chard, spinach, and kale, as well as nuts, wheat, and tropical fruits.

- **Fiber:** This nutrient, found in whole grains, flax, certain cereals, beans, and vegetables, has been shown to reduce estrogen levels, which in turn can slow the growth of cancer cells in the breasts. When shopping, swap your white bread with whole grain bread, your white rice with brown rice, and your sugary cereal for a cereal rich in fiber and the vitamins listed above.

- **Fruits and Vegetables:** In general, fruits and vegetables carry the vitamins and nutrients that can help lower your risk of developing breast and ovarian cancer. Aim for at least five servings a day, and try to include lots of cruciferous vegetables, like broccoli and cauliflower, and dark, leafy greens, like kale and spinach.

CHAPTER 7

ADDITIONAL FACTORS

Breastfeeding

Breastfeeding for one to two years has been proven to reduce your estrogen levels, which may lower your risk of developing breast cancer. (This is especially true if you have a family history of the disease.) Breastfeeding also offers many health benefits to babies and may reduce a female baby's overall risk of developing breast cancer later in life.

Environmental Factors

With more scientific evidence emerging every day, it's clear that the chemicals in our environment play a role in altering our biological processes. We now know that our exposures to toxic chemicals, polluted air, and radiation are connected to our breast cancer risk. But because the environment is so complex, it is difficult to determine precisely which factor—or factors—leads to breast cancer, both the most common cancer and the leading cause of cancer deaths among women worldwide.

Some of the risk factors for breast cancer, such as our family history, can't be helped. But we can control particular environmental factors. Get to know the chemicals that have been linked to breast cancer and learn about what you can do in terms of personal, corporate, and political action to limit your exposure, thereby reducing your risk of breast cancer.

Emotions, Personality, and Cancer

Over the last 20 years, a large amount of research has shown that emotions and mental outlook can affect a person's resistance to ovarian cancer. Being depressed, suffering from grief, and holding in anger may weaken the body's ability to resist cancer, particularly if you have a passive-aggressive personality. Additionally, cancers may be brought on by stressful events that happen in life, which can add to the risk of getting cancer. Other studies have also shown the more severe the depression, the higher the rate of death from cancer.

However, there is no definitive proof that negative emotions and stress directly cause cancer. Rather, they affect the immune system, which is what ties them to prevention. Whenever the immune system is weakened, especially from stress, poor diet, or pollutants, an environment for cancer growth can develop. Women with spreading breast or ovarian cancer and a meek personality type were shown to have a shorter survival rate than women who were able to show their anger.

Meanwhile, women who believed they would not let the cancer beat them have been shown to have longer cancer-free periods and an overall longer survival rate compared to passive women.

Stress and Cancer

Modern life is exhausting. The extra demands of going to school, getting and keeping a job, running a household, and being active in the community extend our days and shorten our nights, wearing us down. And many of us take care of everyone else at the expense of our own needs.

Ongoing stress and sleep deprivation raise serious concerns about our overall health and risks for breast or ovarian cancers. Extra stress leads to higher blood pressure levels and increases in the stress hormone cortisol, which can negatively affect our immune system's ability to function properly and protect our cells from injury. We need quality sleep to function well, keep our immune system strong, and repair and heal the wear and tear of everyday life.

Relaxing your mind may also protect you against cancer. Getting enough rest helps the immune system during stressful times. Meditation and meditative activities may also help. Any time you can bring down your anxiety level through methods like meditation and relaxation, you are better able to handle the difficulties of deciding what treatment routes to take. When you lower your anxiety levels, your mind can react in a calmer and more normal manner.

Studies show that meditation helps lower anxiety, depression, discomfort, and pain. As a patient's moods improve, there are lower levels of stress hormones that weaken the immune system. Patients with advanced cancer show stabilization or even a slight decrease in tumor size and extent after meditation.

However, it has never actually been proven that meditation can prevent or treat cancer. Still, there is little doubt of the benefits of mediation as an adjunct to cancer treatment, allowing the patient to feel in control of the stresses that cancer and cancer treatment can bring.

CHAPTER 8

HOW CAN WE PROTECT OUR DAUGHTERS FROM BREAST CANCER?

Avoiding early puberty

Established risk factors for breast cancer include early age at menarche (first period), which increases premenopausal cumulative estrogen exposure. A diet rich in fruits and vegetables with high vitamin A content has been found to delay sexual maturation and carcinogen-induced mammary tumors in rats. On the other hand, consumption of high-carbohydrate drinks (i.e. soft drinks or soda), processed meats, and shellfish during childhood are all associated with early puberty in girls.

Some personal care products have also been found to cause sexual maturation in girls (and feminization, including breast growth, in boys). These include shampoo and other hair products, body creams, body oils, and various personal care products that contain lavender or tea tree oil.

Furthermore, personal products containing parabens are suspected of contributing to the development of breast cancer. These products are intended for external use but are often absorbed through the skin or scalp. In addition, there are a number of hair care and other products marketed to African American women that contain placenta or "hormone" that should be avoided.

Childhood milk consumption and breast cancer

Although milk consumption during adulthood is associated with a higher risk of breast cancer, milk has previously been found to protect against breast cancer when consumed in infancy and childhood. A partial explanation for this finding is that the milk contains calcium and vitamin D, both of which are known to protect against breast cancer. Exposure to estrogen during childhood also appears to protect against subsequent breast cancer, although the mechanism of action is not understood. Milk consumption is also associated with higher bone mineral density and other measures of bone health.

Based on the available evidence, milk starts to increase risk in American girls during late adolescence. We recommend organic milk (from grass-fed cows, if possible), but not raw milk, for children's consumption. Much of the milk we drink today is produced from pregnant cows in which estrogen and progesterone levels are markedly elevated. Non-organic milk contains an additional recombinant bovine growth hormone zeranol and other additives administered to cows and sheep.

Childhood weight and breast cancer

Established risk factors for breast cancer also include a tall stature, which is associated with higher levels of growth hormones. However, weight should not be confused with height. While obesity is associated with an increased risk of postmenopausal breast cancer in adult women, being somewhat overweight appears to be protective against breast cancer before menopause.

This is true also of childhood. Girls should not be deprived of needed calories in an effort to delay puberty. Additionally, tall, thin girls go on to have the highest rates of premenopausal breast cancer. However, one study found that associating childhood height and weight with an increased risk of breast cancer held only for women without a family history of the disease.

Childhood exercise and breast cancer

There is some evidence that vigorous exercise during childhood reduces the risk of breast cancer, although evidence for this is strongest in teenagers and women. This is for two reasons: evidence shows that adequate amounts of vitamin D prevent breast cancer, and exercise can help prevent early puberty. Thus, based on the available evidence, it makes sense for our high-risk daughters to participate in outdoor sports and other regular physical activities during childhood. Although it is important to take steps to avoid sunburn, girls should be allowed to regularly expose their skin to sunlight. This includes African Americans and other girls of color.

Breasts take over ten years to fully develop. Everyone grows at her own pace, and breast development can stop, start, and stop again. Breasts actually begin developing while you are a tiny three-week-old fetus in your mom's uterus. Later, they go through a phase of rapid growth and development during puberty, most of which occurs during a four-year period. Your breasts grow and change a little more after high school and don't actually reach their full size until you're 25.

It's really important that girls and young teens make healthy lifestyle choices when their breasts are growing and changing the most. Growing breast tissue is more sensitive than that of fully developed breasts. This means that what we eat and drink, the air we breathe, the environmental toxins to which we are exposed, and the amount of exercise we get while our breasts are growing and changing become the foundation for our newly forming breast tissue.

Getting breast cancer when you are a teenager or young adult is extremely rare. Breast cancers are mostly diagnosed in women over 50. But, in your teens and 20s, you're developing lifelong behaviors. Making the following healthy habits a part of your life can reduce your risk of getting breast cancer in the long run:

Move it! Compared to no physical activity, exercising five hours a week can substantially reduce your risk.

Bike, run, dance, walk your dog, jump on the bed. They're all good.

Toss the fries! Opt for a low-fat, high-fiber diet that includes lots of fruits and veggies. Also, try to limit red meat and animal fat, and choose olive oil instead of vegetable or canola oil.

Butt out! Smoking kills people! Get help quitting.

Stay fit! Maintain a healthy body weight. We know this means something different to everyone, but keep in mind that extra fat cells make extra estrogen, which can increase your risk.

Be happy! There's no proven link between stress and breast cancer, but reducing it can improve your quality of life. Keep a positive attitude, learn to relax, and maintain your emotional health.

CHAPTER 9

~~~~~~~~~~~~~~~~~~~~~~~~~~~~~~~~~~~~~

TEN FOODS THAT CAN REDUCE THE RISK OF BREAST & OVARIAN CANCERS

Using Food as Medicine

Diet is extremely influential in preventing and healing breast and ovarian cancers. Beyond consuming an abundant variety of fresh produce and limiting dairy, meat, and sugar, certain foods specifically target breast and ovarian cancer cells, demonstrating extraordinary success in defeating these life-threatening diseases.

Curry

The spice that gives curry its beautiful yellow color contains a chemical called curcumin. Lab studies using curcumin supplements have shown that it might play a role in fighting breast cancer tumors when combined with certain drug-based therapy. It also might have an anti-inflammatory effect that could protect your overall health. You'll need supplements to get enough curcumin, but a diet of veggie curry full of broccoli, onions, and garlic can help make your anti-cancer nutrition plan more fun.

Broccoli

Broccoli has garnered the most attention as a breast cancer prevention food. Research has shown that it blocks tumor growth, preventing the further spread of cancer if it begins. You can get the same anti-cancer benefit from other cruciferous veggies, including cauliflower, cabbage, Brussels sprouts, and kale, but you most likely need to eat one or more of these vegetables every day.

Apples

An apple a day may keep breast cancer away, but there's a catch. If you normally peel your apple and toss away the colorful wrapping, you're also tossing away a rich source of antioxidants, fiber, and other compounds needed for anti-cancer nutrition. Lab studies show that an apple peel can actually fight the spread of cancer cells. The good news is that you don't need exotic varieties—the research came from readily available Gala apples—so add them to your breast cancer prevention shopping list.

Pomegranates

Research into the role of pomegranates is in its early stages, but a cell culture study suggests that the fruit contains a compound that might help fight cancer growth, especially estrogen-dependent cancers. Pomegranates make a delicious and healthy addition to any breast cancer management plan or breast cancer prevention diet, in either fruit or juice form. Adding them to your grocery list may also benefit others in your family, in that they fight heart disease and prostate cancer.

Walnuts

Get out your nutcracker! Walnuts contain many helpful nutrients and healthy omega-3 fatty acids, which help your body fight inflammation. Research also suggests that walnuts may slow the growth of breast cancer tumors, so this tasty nut could play a role in breast cancer management even after diagnosis.

Fish

Other great sources of omega-3 fatty acids include certain fish and fish oils. Fish is also an excellent source of lean protein and a great addition to a breast cancer prevention plan because it limits your intake of red meat and processed meats, such as bacon and packaged deli meats, which is recommended to reduce your cancer risk. Opt for salmon, mackerel, sea bass, and tuna.

Flaxseed

Shopping for healthy fats will inevitably lead you to flaxseed oil, but this is an instance in which your best anti-cancer nutrition choice is the seed itself, ground into a flour-like dust. When you use milled flaxseed, it has a component called lignans, which may decrease cancer growth, making it perfect for a breast cancer management diet. You can buy ground flaxseed or grind the seeds yourself using a coffee grinder. Then, sprinkle the flaxseed on salads or include it in muffins.

Orange Fruits and Vegetables

When it comes to breast cancer prevention, consider eating more carrots, cantaloupe, and sweet potatoes, all foods rich in the form of vitamin A known as carotenoids. Orange vegetables and fruits are most often held up as sources of this powerful compound for breast cancer prevention. If you want to amp up the carotenoids in your breast cancer diet, make sure you get lots of orange, red, yellow, and even dark green foods.

Green Tea

Drinking a mere two cups per day of green tea can slash your risk of ovarian cancer by half. Researchers followed 61,057 women, ranging from 40 to 76 years of age, over the course of 15 years. For those who drank one cup of green tea daily, the risk of ovarian cancer was reduced by 24 percent, while two or more cups lowered the risk by 46 percent. Women who consumed the beverage consistently for over 30 years saw a reduction in ovarian cancer rates by nearly 75 percent. Scientists believe the high levels of antioxidants found in green tea are responsible for the results. Not only do these powerful phytonutrients help prevent and repair DNA damage, but they also hinder the growth and spread of cancer cells by increasing apoptosis.

Ginger

Ginger root is an outstanding food for annihilating ovarian cancer cells. When researchers dissolved ginger powder in a solution containing ovarian cancer cultures, the mutant cells died. Ginger destroys ovarian cancer cells in two ways: apoptosis, a process of cellular self-destruction, and autophagy, where the cells digest themselves. Ginger root also controls inflammation, a precursor to ovarian cancer.

CHAPTER 10

〜〜〜〜〜〜〜〜〜〜〜〜〜〜〜〜〜〜〜〜〜〜〜〜〜〜〜

HOW TO GET THE MOST OF YOUR DOCTOR VISIT

As the old saying goes, prevention is the best medicine, so it's important to keep regular appointments, in which you talk about what you've noticed, and get screened for diseases and illnesses.

Before your appointment, it's best to prepare not only with the information you'll need to provide your doctor, but to also come with a list of questions to take full advantage of your doctor's knowledge. Here's a handy guide that should help you get ready for your visit.

What to bring

You don't necessarily have to bring anything physical to your appointment, aside from your health insurance card. But unless you have everything memorized, it may help to create a couple of lists.

- List all of the medications you're taking, whether they're over-the-counter drugs, prescription medicines, vitamins, or other supplements.

- Be prepared to tell your doctor about your medical history (including your family medical history), allergies, and past and current health conditions.

What to ask yourself before you go

It helps to do a little self-evaluation before your appointment. To get a handle on what you should ask your health care provider, ask yourself questions like:

- Do I have any concerns or symptoms that I should bring up?

- How can I best describe these issues to my health care provider?

- How long have I been experiencing these symptoms or concerns?

- Have I started taking any new medications or supplements?

- Are there any tests or medications that I'd like to know more about?

What to ask your health care provider

Preparing yourself with a list of questions before your appointment can ensure that all the important topics are addressed. Here are a few to start with, but don't hesitate to ask more if you need clarification or think of something else.

- Do I need any routine tests or screenings, like a mammogram, Pap test, sexually transmitted disease tests, osteoporosis screening, colonoscopy, or blood test?

- Do I have any new moles or suspicious spots on my skin?

- What treatments are recommended for the concerns or conditions I have? Are there particular benefits or risks?

- What are the side effects I should watch out for when taking the medications you've prescribed?

- Are there any additional resources that I can check out to learn more about my medications, issues, or conditions?

- Do I need a referral for a different kind of health care provider?

- Should I schedule a follow-up visit?

You should also ask your health care provider any questions you have about sleep habits, stress management, exercise regimens, diets, birth control, and family planning. He or she can help you decide what's best for you.

After the appointment, be sure to keep your health care provider informed about any symptom changes, and don't be afraid to get back in touch with additional questions or concerns. Keep your follow-up visit and do your best to follow your health care provider's recommendations and advice.

CHAPTER 11

〜〜〜〜〜〜〜〜〜〜〜〜〜〜〜〜〜〜〜〜〜〜〜〜〜〜〜〜〜

LIVING BEYOND BREAST OR OVARIAN CANCER

Services to Think About

Talk with your doctor to help locate services such as these:

Individual Counseling

Trained mental health specialists can help you deal with your feelings, such as anger, sadness, and concern for your future.

Couples Counseling

You and your partner can work with trained specialists who will talk about your problems, learn about your needs, and find ways to cope. Counseling may also include issues related to sex and intimacy.

Faith or Spiritual Counseling

Some members of the clergy are trained to help you cope with your cancer concerns, such as feeling alone, fearing death, searching for meaning, and doubting your faith.

Family Support Programs

Your whole family may be involved in the healing process. In these programs, you and your family members take part in therapy sessions with trained specialists who can help you talk about problems, learn about each other's needs, and find answers.

Genetic Counseling

Trained specialists can advise you on whether you should have genetic testing for cancer and how you can deal with the results. It can be helpful for you and for family members who have concerns about their own health.

Home Care Services

State and local governments offer many services that you may find useful after cancer treatment. For example, a nurse or physical therapist may be able to come to your home. You may also be able to get help with housework or cooking. Check the phonebook under the categories social services, health services, or aging services.

Long-Term Follow-up Clinics

All doctors can offer follow-up care, but there are also clinics that specialize in long-term follow-up care after cancer. These clinics most often see people who are no longer being treated by an oncologist and who are considered free of disease. Ask your doctor if there are any follow-up cancer clinics in your area.

Occupational Therapists

Occupational therapists can help you regain, develop, and build skills that are important for day-to-day living. They can help you relearn how to do daily activities, such as bathing, dressing, or feeding yourself after cancer treatment.

Nutritionists/Dietitians

Nutritionists and dieticians can help you with gaining or losing weight and with eating well.

Oncology Social Workers

Oncology social workers are trained to counsel you on ways to cope with treatment issues and family problems related to your cancer. They can tell you about resources and connect you with services in your area.

Pain Clinics (also called Pain and Palliative Care Services)

Pain clinics are centers with professionals from many different fields who are specially trained in helping people find relief from pain.

Physical Therapists

Physical therapists are trained to understand how different parts of your body work together. They can teach you about proper exercises and body motions that can help you gain strength and move better after treatment. They can also advise you about proper postures that help prevent injuries.

Quitting Smoking (Smoking Cessation Services)

Research shows that the more support you have in quitting smoking, the greater your chance for success. Ask your doctor, nurse, social worker, or hospital about available programs, or call NCI's Smoking Quitline at 1-877-44-U-QUIT (1-877-448-7848).

Speech Therapists

Speech therapists can evaluate and treat any speech, language, or swallowing problems you may have after treatment.

Stress Management Programs

These programs teach ways to relax and take more control over stress. Hospitals, clinics, and local cancer organizations may offer these programs and classes.

Support Groups for Survivors

In-person and online groups enable survivors to interact with others in similar situations.

Survivor Wellness Programs

These types of programs are growing in number, and they are meant for people who have finished their cancer treatment and are interested in redefining their life beyond cancer.

Vocational Rehabilitation Specialists

If you have disabilities or other special needs, these specialists can help you find suitable jobs. They offer services such as counseling, education, and skills training, and they help in obtaining and using assistive technology and tools.

Coping With Fatigue

Here are some ideas:

✓ Plan your day. Be active at the time of day when you feel most alert and energetic.

✓ Take short naps or rest breaks between activities.

✓ Go to sleep and wake up at the same time each day.

✓ Save your energy by changing how you do things. For example, sit on a stool while you cook or wash dishes.

✓ Do what you enjoy, but do less of it. Focus on old or new interests that don't tire you. For example, try to read something brief or listen to music.

✓ Let others help you. They might cook a meal, run errands, or do the laundry. If no one offers, ask for what you need. Friends and family might be willing to help but may not know what to do.

✓ Choose how to spend your energy. Try to let go of things that don't matter as much now.

✓ Think about joining a support group. Talking about your fatigue with others who have had the same problem may help you find new ways to cope.

Pain

Some people have a lot of pain after treatment, while others have less. Everyone is different. Types of pain you may feel after cancer treatment include:

Pain or numbness in the hands and feet due to injured nerves - Chemotherapy or surgery can damage nerves, which can cause severe pain. For more information on nervous system changes, see Nervous System Changes (Neuropathy).

Painful scars from surgery.

Pain in a missing limb or breast - While doctors don't know why this pain occurs, it is real. It's not just "in your mind." This is sometimes called phantom pain.

Getting Help

Treatment and other health issues, such as arthritis, may be the cause of your pain. If you find that you still have pain after treatment, your doctor can help find the source of your pain and get you relief. You do not have to be in pain. On that note, wanting to control pain is not a sign of weakness. It's a way to help you feel better and stay active.

With your help, your doctor can assess how severe your pain is and may recommend several options.

In most cases, doctors will try the mildest medicines for pain relief first. Then they will work up to stronger ones if needed. The key to getting relief is to take all medicines exactly as your doctor prescribes. To keep pain under control, do not skip doses or wait until you feel pain to take these medicines.

Talking With Your Doctor About Pain

There are different ways to describe your pain to your doctor. They are as follows:

Use numbers. Talk about how strong the pain feels on a scale of 0 to 10, with 0 being no pain and 10 being the worst pain you've ever had.

Describe what the pain feels like. Is it sharp, dull, throbbing, steady?

Point out exactly where it hurts, either on your body or on a drawing. Note whether the pain stays in one place, or whether it moves outward from the spot.

Explain when you feel pain. Note when it starts, how long it lasts, if it gets better or worse at certain times of the day or night, and if anything you do makes it better or worse.

Describe how your pain affects your daily life. Does it keep you from working? Doing household chores? Seeing friends and family? Going out and having fun?

Make a list of all the medicines you take (for any reason). If you take anything for pain relief, how much do they help?

Talk about side effects you have from your pain-control medicine, such as constipation, changes in bowel habits, or feeling groggy or "out of it." Many of these problems can be helped.

Keep a record of your pain. Jotting down notes about your pain can help you track changes over time. It can also show how you respond to any pain control medicine or other treatment you receive.

Mouth or Teeth Problems

Many people who have been treated for cancer develop problems with their mouth or teeth. Some problems go away after treatment. Others last a long time, while some never go away. Some problems develop months or years after your treatment has ended.

Radiation or surgery to the head and neck can cause problems with your teeth and gums; the soft, moist lining of your mouth; glands that make saliva (spit); and jawbones. If you were treated with certain types of chemotherapy, you may also have these problems. This can cause:

✓ Dry mouth

✓ Cavities and other kinds of tooth problems

✓   Loss of or change in sense of taste

✓   Painful mouth and gums

✓   Infections in your mouth

✓   Jaw stiffness or jawbone changes

Who Has These Problems?

Almost all people who have had radiation therapy to the head and neck/

Most people who have had bone marrow transplants/

About two out of every five people treated with chemotherapy/

Preventing or Relieving Mouth or Teeth Problems

Keep your mouth moist.

Drink a lot of water.

Suck on ice chips.

Chew sugarless gum or suck on sugar-free hard candy.

Use a saliva substitute to help moisten your mouth.

Keep your mouth clean.

Brush your teeth, gums, and tongue with an extra-soft toothbrush after every meal and at bedtime. If it hurts, soften the bristles in warm water.

Ask your dentist for tooth sponges, such as Toothettes® or Dentips®, that you can use in place of a toothbrush.

Use mild fluoride toothpaste (like children's toothpaste) and a mouthwash without alcohol.

Floss your teeth gently every day. If your gums bleed or hurt, stay away from areas that are bleeding or sore, but keep flossing your other teeth.

Rinse your mouth several times a day with a solution of 1/4 teaspoon baking soda and 1/8 teaspoon salt in 1 cup of warm water. Follow with a plain water rinse.

If you have dentures, clean, brush, and rinse them after meals. Have your dentist check them to make sure they still fit you well.

If your mouth is sore, remember to stay away from:

Sharp, crunchy foods, like chips, which can scrape or cut your mouth

Foods that are hot, spicy, or high in acid, like citrus fruits and juices, which can irritate your mouth

Sugary foods, like candy or soda, which can cause cavities

Toothpicks, which can cut your mouth

All tobacco products

Alcoholic drinks

Body Changes and Intimacy

Many survivors don't want people to see the effects of treatment like scars, skin changes, loss of limbs, and changes in weight. Even if your treatment isn't visible to others, your body changes may trouble you. Feelings of anger and grief are natural. Additionally, feeling bad about your body can lower your sex drive. This loss of, or reduction in, your sex life may make you feel even worse about yourself.

Changes in the way you look can also be hard for your loved ones, which can be hard on you. Parents and grandparents often worry about how they look to a child or grandchild. They fear that changes in their appearance may scare the child or get in the way of getting close.

How do you cope with body changes?

Mourn your losses. They are real, and you have a right to grieve.

Try to focus on the ways that coping with cancer has made you stronger, wiser, and more realistic.

If you find that your skin has changed from radiation, ask your doctor about ways you can care for it.

Look for new ways to enhance your appearance. A new haircut, hair color, brand of makeup, or piece of clothing may give you a lift.

If you choose to wear a breast form (prosthesis), make sure it fits you well. Your health insurance plan may also pay for it.

Try to recognize that you are more than your cancer. Know that you have worth, no matter how you look or what happens to you in life.

Changes in Sex Life

You may have changes in your sex life after cancer treatment. Many people do. Depending on the cancer you had, these problems may be short-term or long-term. For example, about half of women who have had long-term treatment for breast and reproductive organ cancers, and more than half of men treated for prostate cancer, report long-term sexual problems. Many cancer survivors say they were not prepared for the changes in their sex lives.

Sexual problems after cancer treatment are often caused by changes to your body from surgery, chemotherapy, or radiation, or by the effects of certain medicines. Sometimes emotional issues can be the cause of sexual problems. Some examples include anxiety, depression, feelings of guilt about what contributed to your cancer, changes in body image after surgery, and stress between you and your partner. Your past sex life is not related to your current sexual problems.

So,what types of sexual problems occur? People report these main concerns:

Worrying about intimacy after treatment. Some may struggle with their body image after treatment. Even thinking about being seen without clothes may be stressful. People may worry that having sex will hurt, that they won't be able to perform, or that they will feel less attractive. Pain, loss of interest, depression, or cancer medicines can also affect sex drive.

Not being able to have sex as you did before. Some cancer treatments cause changes in sex organs that also change your sex life.

Some women find it harder, or even painful, to have sex after cancer treatment. Some cancer treatments can cause these problems; sometimes, there is no clear cause. Some women also lose sensation in their genital area.

Having menopause symptoms. When women stop getting their periods, they can get hot flashes, dryness or tightness in the vagina, and other problems that can affect their desire to have sex.

Losing the ability to have children. Some cancer treatments can cause infertility, making it impossible for cancer survivors to have children. For others, depending on the type of treatment, the person's age, and the length of time since treatment, having children may still be   possible.

SURVIVOR STORIES

SHETABIA MORGAN-PUTMAN

of Clarkston, Georgia

Ovarian Cancer Survivor

~~~~~~

Baby, my back is hurting me so bad," I explained to my husband. He told me to come and lie down and rest. It was Christmas Eve and I was looking out the window. It was raining and I was debating if I was going to church. My back was aching so badly I decided to go to bed. As I'm lying there, it started stinging worse, like needles on my side. I put up with the pain until the 12th hour of Christmas Eve 2009, and finally I just woke my husband up and said, "Honey, I can't take this pain anymore, please take me to the emergency room!"

As we proceeded to leave the house, we were arguing about what hospital I was going to, and he insisted on Emory. I had never been to Emory and never thought my insurance would take Emory, but he didn't care and was more adamant about going. As I was lying in the bed in the emergency room, I noticed how bloated my stomach was and I kept telling my husband, I'm probably getting ready to get my cycle or have a urinary tract infection. The nurse came in and asked all kinds of medical questions. The main ones were, "Do you have kids? Are you trying to get pregnant?" I answered "no" and "yes." Yes, we were trying to get pregnant, but to have intercourse just wasn't feeling right. It felt like someone was ramming a stick up me, it became so painful. We also told the nurse we were going to get married that Monday after New Year's Day, which was January 4, 2010. So the nurse said, "That's wonderful and congratulations, but I'm going to have to take a CT scan to see what is going on." So my husband and I looked at each other and said, "What is a CT scan?" The nurse explained that I would have to drink this white contrast and then shoot die into my body to see what the problem is.

She proceeded to say it's not as painful as you think. So we agreed to do it, so we can get back to trying to make a baby, both of us laughing. The nurse wheeled me around to the CT scan room, me not having a worry in the world, just ready for them to give me something for pain so I can go home. After the CT scan, she rolled me back to the room, and my husband and I started playing games and joking. We called my mom because we were supposed to be at a family breakfast, but I told my mom I was at the emergency room and not to worry. We would be leaving soon, but we wouldn't make the breakfast.

She panicked and came to the hospital anyway. Soon the nurse came back with the results, and it was heart wrenching. Ms. Morgan, you have two tumors on your ovaries, one the size of a grapefruit and the other one the size of an orange! All of the conversation stopped between my mom, my husband, and me. You could hear a pin drop. So I said, "Okay, remove the tumors so we can proceed to try to have kids." Then the nurse said, "Ms. Morgan, you don't understand, after we remove the tumors which were causing so much pain when y'all have intercourse, they will have to be tested to see if they are cancerous." I still said, "Okay, let's do it, cause we are getting married on Monday and we want some kids." Then the low blow came. She took the breath out of our bodies. "Ms. Morgan, you won't be able to have kids!" It was dead silence. Tears were rolling down my face and my husband's. She said I would need a total hysterectomy immediately, and she appointed me to the best gynecologic oncologist at Emory specializing in cancer patients, and I was appointed the best oncologist at Emory. Before I go on, let me tell you about my husband Terrell.

We met at my best friends' birthday party, which was on a Monday, January 22, 2009. We hit it off so well it was like a breath of fresh air for the both of us. We had been in crazy relationships previously, and it was just good to meet someone who was the same level in life as you are. Our first date lasted approximately 11 hours straight, just talking about any and everything. Oh my heart was beating so fast because I had just gotten out of a previous relationship with this abusive guy, but the guy kept lingering around like a stray cat. I was so afraid that Terrell would not want to have anything to do with my drama until I had closed that chapter of my life. So finally I had to get a restraining order against the ex-boyfriend and had him locked up in order for him to leave me alone. I was so blessed to have Terrell by my side, but it was up to me to call the police, just so he would know that I was sincere about moving on and ending that chapter of my relationship with the devil.

After that, things went smoothly and we saw each other everyday when I got off work. We were inseparable. We dated for about a year, and he started talking about marrying me. I was so nervous because I would have never thought I would be getting married after being in an abusive relationship. His mom told him he was moving too fast, and my mother said the same thing. We both explained that we had been through so many relationships and we weren't getting any younger, and we both knew what exactly what we wanted. He was my soul mate, my best friend, and my confidant. It seems like we were meant to be. We both knew God put us together for a reason. He was 100 percent in my corner about everything. He proposed to me in November of 2009. So we set the date to be on January 4, 2010. We didn't want a wedding, but a big reception. So we started planning for the reception in December of 2009.

By the end of December of 2009, New Years Eve to be exact, I started to experience the pain on my side and in my back, which brought us back to the emergency room at Emory. I was so scared of losing Terrell because we were just told we couldn't have kids and I had to have a hysterectomy, plus I had to have these tumors removed and they may be cancerous. Terrell was by my side the whole time, not even mentioning he was leaving. We did discuss the courthouse, and we both agreed that Monday, January 4th, would be the day. I was so happy and scared at the same time knowing my life was getting ready to change, meaning I might have cancer and my last name won't be the same. It was a huge step for the both of us. The day arrived and we got married, then we went to the doctor's office to set up the surgery. The doctor couldn't believe that we had just gotten married. My husband had gotten over the fact that we couldn't have kids, just as long as I was healthy. They performed the surgery and I was diagnosed with Ovarian Cancer Stage IIIc. It was silent in the room, and I kept seeing faces of disbelief. I kept asking everybody, "Why are y'all looking like that?" Then the doctor came in. It still didn't sink in when I was at the hospital until the doctors said I had to do chemotherapy. Then it hit me. The room was dark, and all I can imagine is I just got married to the soulmate of my life, please God, don't take him away from me.

I cried and prayed at the same time because I knew my life would never be the same. I have been fighting ovarian cancer since 2010, been in remission for one year, and then in 2011, it came back. Then I beat it again in 2012. It came back in 2013. I was in remission for 6 months, and now I'm fighting as we speak. I had never even heard of ovarian cancer, let alone know the symptoms. I do know my grandmother passed from ovarian cancer at the age of 84. I wasn't aware of the BRCA gene test. If I had known what I know now, I probably would have saved my own life... literally! I did get my regular Pap smear checkups. I knew when the ball was dropped, but didn't have the heart to tell my parents.

I was too cheap to pay the $300 for the ultrasound when I was in so much pain from my side. Yep, that's what my ob/gyn wanted: $300.00. I knew it was my fault, and I had to speak up fast. So, unexpectedly, on the night I was in the hospital trying to come up with a plan to tell my mom, I see this tall guy with pearly white teeth walk in my room. It was my uncle, my mom's brother. I was crying so badly, and he asked me what was wrong? I told the situation about the $300, and that I was too cheap to pay for an ultrasound and the cancer could have been prevented. Also, I told him my mom is gonna call the ob/gyn and let her know the legal action for negligence will be brought against her. I told my uncle it wasn't the doctor's fault, it was my fault, and I didn't have the guts to tell her. So he agreed to tell her and told me everything was gonna be okay. So I asked him, "Why did it have to be me to get cancer?" He responded, "Why not you?" You are one of His soldiers on the battlefield and He knows who can fight and be winner." That stuck with me until this very day, as I often keep asking "why me?" So I always remember because I am the soldier for the Lord. I won't give up this fight because I'm afraid of disappointing God. He has a huge purpose for me being on this earth, and I'm gonna enjoy every minute of it. My motto is: ALWAYS MAKE IT COUNT! Don't Judge "UNTEAL" you know my story!!

LADIES, LADIES, LADIES. PLEASE GET CHECKED OUT. DO NOT LET $300.00 COME BETWEEN YOU AND YOUR HEALTH. IF I WOULD HAVE GOTTEN THE ULTRASOUND... WOULDA, SHOULDA, COULDA... GO GET CHECKED!

Shetabia

DAWN SMITH

of Landover, Maryland

Breast Cancer Survivor

~~~~~~

My journey as a Breast Cancer Warrior/Thriver! I was diagnosed with Triple Negative Metaplastic breast cancer, a rare and aggressive form of breast cancer, in May 2010 at the age of 49. It was Grade 3, Stage 2B. My tumor did not express the gene receptors for estrogen, progesterone, or HER2 neu (Human Epidermal Growth Factor Receptor 2) protein, which is how I was classified as a Triple Negative, which statistically affects black women in greater numbers.

I found my lump on my left breast, a hard round mass larger than a quarter, on a Sunday on my last day of vacation in Florida, nine months after my yearly mammogram. I was going to call the doctor the following day, but decided to call as soon as we made it home. Although there was no history of breast cancer in my immediate family, in my heart, I knew this was something serious. I saw my gynecologist the next day, and she had an alarming look on her face and said, "Yes, this definitely was something that needed further attention." The next day, I had a mammogram and a sonogram. Afterwards, the tech returned and summoned my husband and stated the radiologist wanted to review the scans with us, which confirmed my thoughts of it being a benign cancer. A biopsy was scheduled and performed days later.

I received the conformation call four days after my biopsy, on our way to the store. I turned to my husband and said, "It's cancer." He stared at me for a moment in disbelief, we continued on our way, and we had dinner afterwards. I was not alarmed, as I knew from the day that I found my lump that it was cancer, yet I had no fear at all. I had a thousand questions to ask but had to wait until the next morning for the breast nurse to call. I turned to the Internet that evening to try and research as much as I could about my type of breast cancer, and there was very limited information available. When the breast nurse called, I had plenty of questions waiting for her, from treatments to side effects, to types of medications to upcoming surgeries. You name it, and I asked it.

A lumpectomy was performed along with an axillary lymph node dissection. Seven lymph nodes were removed, and two were positive for cancer. If cancer cells are found in the axillary nodes, it increases the risk of metastatic breast cancer. The lumpectomy revealed that my margins weren't clear and a separate 1cm tumor had grown along with the initial tumor in less than two weeks from my the time of my biopsy to the lumpectomy. The cancer was found on the margin line. I had to decide whether I would have another lumpectomy or a mastectomy. I felt that if it was on the line that they didn't get it all, so I spoke with my husband about my decision and opted for a mastectomy with a DIEP Flap reconstruction. A DIEP flap is a type of breast reconstruction in which blood vessels called Deep Inferior Epigastric Perforators, and the skin and fat connected to them are removed from the lower abdomen and transferred to the chest to reconstruct my breast without the sacrifice of any of the abdominal muscles. My surgery took 15 hours and it was a great decision, as yet another 1 cm tumor had developed and was found within my mastectomy tissue. My cancer (I named it "Lucy") was still trying to spread in my body.

I continued to carry on my journey with a positive mindset to complete four chemotherapy cycles every two weeks of dose dense Adriamycin (The Red Devil) & Cytoxan, then four cycles of Taxol. All were administered through a port (a cath) that was surgically inserted in my chest with attached tubing guided into a neck vein to dispense the drugs. I did lose almost all of my body hair except for a few eyelashes, seven eyebrow hairs on the left and three on the right (yes, I counted them) before it started growing back in. With God's grace, during chemo I never got sick, felt nauseous, fatigued, or lost my sense of taste.

I developed Lymphedema in my left arm as a result of the lymph node removal and neuropathy (numbness, tingling, and pain) in my hands and feet as a side effect during my chemotherapy treatments with Taxol. I have since been diagnosed with Permanent Peripheral Neuropathy in both feet. This is all part of what is referred to as "My New Norm." My body will never be the same as it was prior to cancer.

To this day, I have had a blood transfusion, dealt with mouth sores, radiation burns, hospitalizations due to infections in my left arm, sported a bald head, and endured PET scans, bone scans, CT scans, MRI scans, and Breast MRI Biopsies, all with my head held high and my heart full of joy. I danced (music was playing) into the radiation treatment center on my very first day with the staff looking at me with amazement. They said, "We have a LIVE one!" I laughed and said, "YES YOU DO!" and endured radiation every weekday for 28 days. I actually began to look forward to going to radiation daily, as I counted the days until it ended. I put puzzles together and struck up conversations with the other patients every day while waiting for my turn. On my last day I danced out of the office, jumping up and clicking my heels just before I went out the door.

I had cancer. It didn't have me. I pulled on my Big-Girl panties, put on my boxing gloves, and prepared to fight. Through it all, I realized that God already had a purpose and a plan for me. He has prepared me my whole life with trials and tribulations that made me strong enough to fight this battle with courage, strength, and dignity.

I have met, and continue to meet, many wonderful, strong women, men, survivors, and supporters through support groups, organizations, breast cancer conferences, and retreats throughout this journey. I feel this is why I was diagnosed with breast cancer: to be a voice, to educate others about survivorship, healthier living, and awareness, to guide and be an inspiration to those who have fought before me and are fighting now against this disease. I am honored to become a member of Sisters Network Prince Georges County. I foresee changes in the way breast cancer affects women in Prince Georges County through the education that we provide.

I thank God and my wonderful husband, Vincent, for his unconditional love, prayers, caregiving, support, and understanding throughout this journey in my life. I love you babe! I also thank my many family and friends who have walked this journey with me.

○ ○ ○

This section is from my second diagnosis in August of 2014...

I am truly blessed!!

Tomorrow I am scheduled to have surgery; it has been seven weeks since my previous surgery. Tomorrow I will be having a bilateral oophorectomy—the surgical removal of the ovaries. Removing your ovaries is usually performed to reduce the risk of ovarian cancer, and an oophorectomy can also reduce the risk of breast cancer.

I am sure some are thinking, "Why remove the ovaries if you've already had breast cancer?"

At my one-week follow-up in early August, from my prophylactic (Voluntary) mastectomy, I was informed by my doctors that there was another unexpected cancer that was found and removed. It was DCIS, Ducal Carcinoma In-Situ, Stage 0, it tested positive for estrogen and progesterone. My first cancer was a rare triple negative cancer called Metaplastic.

My surgery team was just as surprised when they got the call from the pathologist asking them which breast had the cancer and informed them that there was a new primary cancer found in my upper quadrant. It's considered a new cancer because the types weren't the same.

You can't imagine how elated and blessed I felt to know that I went with my intuition to try and prevent cancer from returning. I know it wasn't just only my intuition. I had help from God. I have never questioned why I got breast cancer. I have always felt that my diagnosis put me in a position to be one of God's vessels... to encourage, educate, support, inspire, to be a blessing to others and share my testimony... now testimonies with and about breast cancer.

So again, I had to educate myself on DCIS. It's one of the better breast cancers to have, as it is non-invasive and is contained in the ducts. I have no idea how long the cancer was there. I had had a mammogram in October that was clear.

So again, I have no worries of this second diagnosis. I continue to thank God and pray for us all that a cure can be found for all cancers.

I thank my husband, Vincent, for his love and continued support.

Dawn

DEWANDA MITCHELL

of San Bernardino, California

Breast and Ovarian Cancer Survivor

M y name is Dee Mitchell, and I am an ovarian/breast cancer survivor. I have been free from ovarian cancer for almost four years and breast cancer for one year. I am a US Army Veteran, and I am currently employed with the Department of Veterans Affairs in Loma Linda. I was hired in as a Federal VA Police Officer, and now my current position is the Senior Vice President for the American Federation of Government Employees Local 1061 as a Union Advocate.

In April of 2010, I thought I was in good health, besides being a childhood diabetic. I had just turned 47 years old and had started experiencing severe stomach problems. My symptoms included constipation, dizziness, and pelvic pain. I really did not think too much about it at first because I have always had such a busy life.

One day I could hardly move, so I drove myself to the emergency room in Rancho Cucamonga where I they admitted me for a few days.

I had every test in the book done, including an upper and lower GI series, CT Scan, and blood work. While a lot of things were running through my mind, I played over every detail leading up to that point and could remember the bloating of my stomach and how tired I was feeling, which made me feel awful for a long time. At this time, I was not fully aware that these were some of the major symptoms of ovarian cancer.

The first test showed no signs of anything, so I was sent home with medication for the stomach problems. The stomach problems went away for a couple of weeks and the pain came back rapidly. In July 2010, I noticed my stomach was getting larger which indicated there was fluid building inside there. I looked 9 months pregnant! I began to get scared.

I started to remember what my aunt had experienced in 2004 when she was diagnosed with ovarian cancer, and there were some of the same signs I was encountering.

Unfortunately, she passed away the same year. I realized that the women in my family were a high risk factor for ovarian cancer. I was immediately rushed back to a San Antonio emergency room in Rancho Cucamonga, California. The physicians began by emptying the fluids from my stomach, which was very painful. I was then referred to an OB/GYN Physician at Cedar Sinai.

On the following Monday, I was seen by the OB/GYN Physician who conducted a vaginal ultrasound and a CA-125 Blood Test. It took three days for my results to come back. My daughter and I met with the OB.GYN Doctor, and I was informed that my CA-125 was elevated to 800. I was diagnosed with stage 3C ovarian cancer. My mind and body went numb, and I did not know what to say. My daughter started to tear up and stepped in to ask question on my behalf. I asked for a referral to the City of Hope for a second opinion because that was where my Aunt would have gone, but she passed away the day of her appointment.

The first week of May 2010, I met with the GYN/Oncologist at the City Of Hope, who gave me a referral, which was essential for the preparation of my treatment. Similar tests were performed again along with the trans-vaginal ultrasound, and it was confirmed that I had stage 3C ovarian cancer. I was told what my options were, and that I would have to immediately start a treatment plan that consisted of a 6-five hour cycle of aggressive chemo for a total of 18 weeks. This included the chemo medication Taxol and Carboplatin.

I was exhausted, and many times I became sick. I was restless and could not sleep, but I was grateful to be in the hands of the oncologist at the City of Hope.

In the fall of 2010, I was scheduled for surgery. My spirits were high. I was ready to get this over with but still kept myself busy. I had attended my 30-year class reunion the weekend before and had a great time!

I completed a round of radiation treatment because I had reoccurring series of fibroid tumors that were the size of golf balls. I was told that it probably would have been more difficult to do the surgery without a series of radiation treatment.

By this time my hair started to fall out, so I went to the barbershop and had it all cut down short. To this day I still wear it short. September 9, 2010, the day of my surgery, I was really nervous, but I was so grateful because all of my family and friends were in the waiting room at 5:30 in the morning showing their love and support. I felt like a real celebrity that day! My surgery went well, but my recovery was very emotional and difficult. Six weeks of bed rest followed as my journey to recovery began. My sisters, my kids, and my closet friends all took turns to come out and take care of me, and my coworkers held down the fort until I returned. When I went back to my oncologist at the City of Hope after my recovery, my CA-125 had dropped to 275! I was so happy, but the battle has still not been won. Today, I am still taking a chemo maintenance medication called Arimidex.

Subsequently, in April I was diagnosed breast cancer in the right breast. Earlier within that year I had tested positive for the BRCA1 gene. I found out that the official name for this gene is breast cancer 1, early onset. I also learned that women who have been tested positive for either BRCA1 or 2 have a higher risk factor for both breast and ovarian cancers.

Again, I had to endure another six rounds of chemo and had surgery to remove the cancerous tumor on July 22, 2013. This whole experience has motivated me to become a dedicated advocate for the cause of educating the public and finding the cure for ovarian cancer! In 2012, I officially put my support team DIVA4LIFE together that includes family and friends. We have participated in OCC Walk in Studio City, The

Believe Walk in Redlands, CA, The Spirit Walk in Long Beach, CA, and The Run for Her Walk in Pan Pacific Park.

Presently, I am a Board Member for the OASIS of Southern California located in the Inland Empire, and a dedicated Volunteer for OCC (Ovarian Cancer of Coalition of California) located in Studio City, CA.

My ambition and desire is to make this my life-long cause. Today, I spread awareness at healthcare events and public speaking engagements, and I am a speaker for the STS (Survivors Teaching Students) program once a month at the Loma Linda Medical Center in California.

Today, four years after my first diagnosis, I am still standing and staying prayed up! I am thanking God each day for keeping me throughout this experience. I have also truly realized my own strengths. Don't get me wrong... I still suffer with dizziness, tingling in my hands and feet, and constant mood swings, but with the support of my family, friend, and support groups, I am here to see the age of 53! I am truly a DIVA 4 LIFE! This girl is on fire! For the joy of the Lord is my Strength!

Dewanda

CONCLUSION

Today's women are living longer than ever before. On average, women are living nearly 30 years longer than they did a century ago. And while that's good news for us in general, it's not good news for our breasts and ovaries. Aging is the biggest risk factor for breast and ovarian cancers. The longer we live, the more we have to weather the wear and tear of everyday living. Our genes are more likely to develop new harmful mutations and are less able to repair the genetic damage. If important genes stop functioning normally, then abnormal cell growth, such as cancer, is more likely to occur.

Breast and ovarian cancers don't always win! More than 2.5 million women in the United States have beaten breast cancer or are currently in treatment for it. In stage I of ovarian cancer the survival rate is 92 percent. However, only 15 percent of all ovarian cancers are found at this early stage. Thus, early detection is the key, and it will dramatically improve survival rates. Educating women about breast and ovarian cancers is the first step to the cure. If we listen to the whispers and do the proper screening, we can save countless precious lives.

The earlier breast cancer is diagnosed, the better your chances of beating it.

This is why motivating you to know your breasts and to give them some regular TLC is such an important part of breast health awareness and education work. The more familiar you are with how your breasts look and feel, the easier it is for you to notice any unusual changes and have them checked out by your doctor. Being proactive is your key to early diagnosis. The full scope of my breast health awareness and education movement aims to empower young women with all the knowledge they need to reduce their risks and play an active role in their breast cancer journey, from prevention and early detection through recovery and follow-up.

Change is a journey. You have to start somewhere. Whether it's avoiding alcohol and smoking, or rethinking your food choices, roll up your sleeves and get busy. Some changes may be easy to make. Some may feel out of reach. You can only do your best, and you should feel good about your efforts. Whatever first step you take is one in the right direction. One step leads to two steps, and then more.

To one day live in a world without breast and ovarian cancer, it's going to take a movement. You have the power to make and sustain a life-saving difference for yourself, your children, and many others. Your knowledge will help you make the healthiest choices possible. We all want to see an end to breast and ovarian cancers. Spread the word and practice what matters most. Others will follow your lead.

RESOURCES AND SUPPORT

African-American Breast Cancer Alliance

(612) 825-3675

www.aabcainc.org

American Cancer Society

(800) 227-2345

www.cancer.org

Cancer Care – Phone Support

(800) 813-4673

www.cancercare.org

Colletta Orr & Associates

www.CollettaOrr.com

Gynecologic Cancer Foundation

(800) 444-4441

www.thegcf.org or www.wcn.org

Living Beyond Breast Cancer

(855) 807-6386

www.lbbc.org

Ovarian Cancer National Alliance (OCNA)

(202) 331-1332

www.ovariancancer.org

National Coalition for Cancer Survivorship

(877) 622-7937

www.canceradvocacy.org

National Ovarian Cancer Coalition (NOCC)

(888) OVARIAN

www.ovarian.org

Sister's Network, Inc

(866)-781-1808

www.sistersnetworkinc.org

Wellness Community

(888) 793-WELL

www.thewellnesscommunity.org

REFERENCES

http://www.ovariancancerpbc.org/symptoms-and-risks

http://rethinkbreastcancer.com/breast-cancer/think-pink-for-teens/what-you-need-to-know/

http://www.prevention.com/health/health-concerns/ovarian-cancer-prevention-and-diagnosis?page=6

http://www.brightpink.org/awareness-to-action/risk-reduction/

http://www.cancer.org

http://www.minoritynurse.com/article/breast-cancer-finding-roots

http://ovariancancer.about.com/od/preventionscreening/a/ovca_lifestyle.htm

http://foodforbreastcancer.com/articles/how-can-we-protect-our-daughters-from-breast-cancerpercent3F---childhood-and-puberty

http://www.cancer.gov

http://www.nci.gov

ABOUT THE AUTHOR

COLLETTA ORR

is an award-winning research scientist and the CEO of Colletta Orr & Associates. Her interest is in educating women about early diagnosis and ways they can minimize the potential impact of breast and ovarian cancers on their lives. In addition, she wants to educate women about life after breast and ovarian cancers. She is an active member of Voorhees College Washington DC Metropolitan alumni chapter.

She is also a board member of The Washington Inter Alumni Council (WIAC) of UNCF. WIAC is a chapter of The National Alumni Council (NAC), a sponsored organization of UNCF, the United Negro College Fund. She currently serves as the Sergeant-at Arms. Mrs. Orr resides in North Bethedsa, Maryland, with her husband Douglas III and her son Douglas IV.

WE WANT TO HEAR FROM YOU!!!

If this book has made a difference in your life
Colletta would be delighted to hear about it.

Leave a review on Amazon.com!

BOOK COLETTA TO SPEAK AT YOUR NEXT EVENT!

Send an email to booking@publishyourgift.com

Learn more about Colletta at
www.CollettaOrr.com

FOLLOW COLLETTA ON SOCIAL MEDIA

  @CollettaOrr

"EMPOWERING YOU TO IMPACT GENERATIONS"
WWW.PUBLISHYOURGIFT.COM

CPSIA information can be obtained
at www.ICGtesting.com
Printed in the USA
BVOW06s0852100317
478068BV00008B/134/P